# History and Teachings of the Rosicrucians

By W. W. Westcott
Hargrave Jennings
S. L. MacGregor Mathers

Copyright © 2020 Lamp of Trismegistus. All rights reserved. No part of this publication may be reproduced or transmitted in any form or by any means, electronic or mechanical, including photocopying, recording, or by any information storage and retrieval system, without permission in writing from Lamp of Trismegistus. Reviewers may quote brief passages.

ISBN: 978-1-63118-487-1

*Esoteric Classics*

## Other Books in this Series and Related Titles

*Rosicrucian Rules, Secret Signs, Codes and Symbols* by various (978-1-63118-488-8)

*The Rosicrucian Chemical Marriage* by Christian Rosenkreuz (978-1-63118-458-1)

*Masonic and Rosicrucian History* by M P Hall & H Voorhis (978-1-63118-486-4)

*Rosicrucians and Speculative Masonry in the Seventeenth Century* (978-1-63118-489-5)

*Qabbalistic Teachings and the Tree of Life* by M P Hall (978-1-63118-482-6)

*The Kabbalah of Masonry & Related Writings* by E Levi &c (978-1-63118-453-6)

*The Sepher Yetzirah and the Qabalah* by M P Hall (978-1-63118-481-9)

*Confessions of an English Opium-Eater* by T De Quincey (978-1-63118-485-7)

*The Poem of Hashish* by A Crowley & C Baudelaire (978-1-63118-484-0)

*Fortune-Telling with Dice* by Astra Cielo (978-1-63118-466-6)

*History, Analysis and Secret Tradition of the Tarot* by Hall &c (978-1-63118-445-1)

*Crystal Vision Through Crystal Gazing* by Achad (978-1-63118-455-0)

*Ancient Mysteries and Secret Societies* by M P Hall (978-1-63118-410-9)

*The Secrets of Enoch* by Enoch (978-1-63118-449-9)

*The Gospel of the Nativity of Mary* by St. Matthew (978-1-63118-448-2)

*Buddhist Psalms* by Shinran (978-1-63118-465-9)

*The Path of Light: A Manual of Maha-Yana Buddhism* (978-1-63118-471-0)

*Arcane Formulas or Mental Alchemy* by W W Atkinson (978-1-63118-459-8)

*The Machinery of the Mind* by Dion Fortune (978-1-63118-451-2)

*The Leadbeater Reader: A Selection of Occult Essays* (978-1-63118-483-3)

*The Human Aura: Astral Colors and Thought Forms* (978-1-63118-419-2)

**Audio versions are also available on Audible, Amazon and Apple**

# Table of Contents

Introduction...7

*Rosicrucians: Their History and Aims*
By William Wynn Westcott...9

*The Rosicrucian and Hermetic Brethren*
By Hargrave Jennings...29

*Rosicrucian Thoughts on the Ever-Burning Lamps of the Ancients*
By William Wynn Westcott...37

*The True Rosicrucian Order*
By Samuel Liddell MacGregor Mathers...55

*The Rosicrucians*
By William Wynn Westcott...59

# INTRODUCTION

The word "esoteric" can be difficult to define. Esotericism in general can be seen less as a system of beliefs and more as a category, which encompasses numerous, different systems of beliefs. It's a bit of juxtaposition, since the word "esoteric" indicates something that few people know about, while the term itself broadly covers numerous philosophies, practices, areas of study and belief systems.

In a greater sense, Esotericism acts as a storehouse for secret knowledge, which is often considered ancient (by *tradition, if not by fact),* passed down from generation to generation, in private. At various times in history, simply possessing the knowledge of some of these subjects, was considered illegal and a jailable offence, if discovered. This usually included such general topics as Alchemy, Pharmacology, Qabalah, Hermeticism, Occultism, Ceremonial Magic, Astrology, Divination, Rosicrucianism and so on. Collectively, these areas of study were often referred to as the esoteric sciences.

Sometimes, the outer garment of a subject isn't esoteric, while what is hidden beneath it, is. As an example, Freemasonry isn't necessarily esoteric by nature (at *least not anymore),* but certain signs, passwords and handshakes given to the candidate during their initiation, are in fact, esoteric, in the sense that they are hidden from the general public.

Today, in the twenty-first century, such topics are readily available at bookstores across the country, and numerous mainsteam publishers offer beginners guides and coffee-table volumes on many of these subjects, intended for mass appeal. Books like *"The Secret"* have turned previously arcane topics into household knowledge. All that being the case, however, it isn't to say that there still aren't buried secrets to uncover, ancient wisdom being ignored and forgotten mysteries to be explored. In fact, it is often that we are only able to further our own studies by standing on the shoulders of these disappearing giants.

Lamp of Trismegistus is doing its part to help preserve humanity's esoteric history by making some of these classics available to those students who are seeking to unearth the knowledge of these ancient colossi.

So, be sure to check other titles from our *Esoteric Classics* series, as well as our *Occult Fiction*, *Theosophical Classics*, *Foundations of Freemasonry Series*, *Supernatural Fiction*, *Paranormal Research Series*, *Studies in Buddhism* and our *Christian Apocrypha Series*. You can also download the audio versions of most of these titles from Amazon, Apple or Audible, for learning on the go.

# ROSICRUCIANS:
# THEIR HISTORY AND AIMS

## With Reference to the Alleged Connection Between Rosicrucianism & Freemasonry

### By William Wynn Westcott

Brethren, It was with a light heart that I promised our Secretary to prepare a lecture upon the "Rosicrucians, their history and aims, with reference to the alleged connection between Rosicrucianism and Freemasonry." When, however, the time came for the lecture actually to be written, I realized that I had committed one more folly, and that my task was one almost impossible to perform in a satisfactory manner. I was induced to take up this subject because from my connection for many years with the existing Masonic Rosicrucian Society of England, nearly all the available books on the subject had been referred to by me at one time or other, and so it seemed that the materials for such an essay were either well known to me or close at hand. I have given many addresses and lectures on this subject, to Rosicrucians themselves, to Freemasons and to Theosophists, and so I hoped that a satisfactory, although rapid, survey might be designed for your benefit.

Further consideration, however, showed me that however easy it might be to narrate to you the Rosy Cross Legend and to call attention to some notable members of the

Order, the real crux of the matter lay in the difficulty of giving any demonstration of the relations which have existed and do exist — or do exist now for the first time — between Freemasons and those who adopt the name Rosicrucians. A reference to the classical textbook on the *History of Masonry*, by our W. Bro. Past Master Robert Freke Gould, showed me that he had there supplied a full and skillful consideration of the historical aspect of the subject, but I did observe that there was an absence of evidence and arguments along the lines of similarity and diversity of aim, objects and means of action of the two Societies. It is in this direction alone that there seems to be any opportunity for me to say anything novel or beneficial; still, as there are no doubt some of you who have not found time to read up Bro. Gould's chapter on the Rosicrucians, I must include in this lecture an outline of the history of the Founding of the Rosicrucian Order, and must tell you how its existence became known in the beginning of the seventeenth century; I should also relate how the present Masonic Rosicrucians came into existence, and may take this part of the history first.

These latter day representatives of the famous Society of mediaeval Europe are, as I have said, members of the Masonic body, Master Masons of necessity, and I must confess that they have carried into the Society a proportion of the calm and dignified satisfaction with existence, which has always marked the Freemason. Our Lodge is almost alone in spending time in worrying out our origin, not to say destiny, while thousands of Lodges around us pass their periods of existence in the holy calm of benevolence and mutual admiration, and their only sign of activity is in the time of refreshment. So among my *quasi Rosicrucian fratres* there are only a minority who make any attempt to solve the mystery of even the recent origin of the *Soc. Ros. in Ang.*, and still less of the origin of the Society attributed to the German sage of *anno domini* 1450. Although somewhat incurious as to their origin, I must confess with pleasure that the Rosicrucians over whom I rule, — three great Colleges besides lesser groups — do pay considerable attention to the declared aims of the Society, which are stated in their Book of Ordinances to be: "*to afford mutual aid and encouragement in working out the great problems of life, and in searching out the Secrets of Nature; to facilitate the study of the system of Philosophy founded upon the Kabbalah and the doctrines of Hermes Trismegistus, which was inculcated by the original Fratres Rosa Crucis of Germany A.D. 1450; and to investigate the meaning and symbolism of all that now remains of the wisdom, art and literature of the Ancient World.*"

Those of you who are prone to scoff, may perhaps find in this confession of aim an opportunity for this process, but I can assure you that although the scope be wide and too ambitious, yet many of its members have filled up voids in the walls of their Temple.

You yourselves, brethren, are pledged to investigate in your Lodges, all " the hidden mysteries of nature and science." This is also a tolerably large Order, and you must confess that it is precious little of it that you do.

The *Soc. Ros. in Anglia* was constituted by the late Robert Wentworth Little, well known as a prominent mason, and

Secretary to the Royal Masonic Institution for Girls, assisted by several other well-known masons, such as Bros. Levander and Dr. Woodman; but the right to the name and the inspiration which set it going was supplied by the late Kenneth R. H. Mackenzie, who, when in Germany in early life, became acquainted with descendants of the old Rosicrucian Fraternity; they admitted him to some lower grades, permitted him, as an experiment, to bring about the formation of an almost exoteric society among Freemasons, and to use the mediaeval German name.

So much for the connection in modern times between Rosicrucians and Freemasons. Let us take one step back, before we go to the origin of the whole matter. In 1830-50 there was in England a similar organization named " Rosicrucian." Godfrey Higgins, the famous antiquarian of Skellow Grange, mentions this College in his great book, "*The Anacalypsis, or an attempt to withdraw the veil from the Saitic Isis.*" This College certainly existed for many years, and a famous city Jewish medical man called Falk, or Dr. Falcon, was for a long period at its head; but I have no evidence that the members of this College were Freemasons, while I have seen proofs that this College was also related to some mystic teachers in Germany who used mottoes instead of proper names, and wrote R.C. after their names, and were as such Rosicrucians, and had descended for some generations from others who also claimed to have been taught and inspired by men who alleged a direct descent from the Fratres Rosae Crucis, whose "*Fama*" or history, when published in 1614, set the whole educated world by the ears.

Modern literature has almost entirely neglected the mediaeval and more ancient religious philosophies, named Theosophia, derived from the Gnostics, the Kabalists, the Hermetics of Alexandria, and the Neo-Platonists. Rosicrucianism was a new presentment of these doctrines, a re-statement of the old positions of Chaldean, Egyptian, and later Greek religious philosophy, in language and form designed by one who had sought out the remnants of these dogmas in their old homes, and had translated them into a new system, and who formed around him a band of earnest students who realized the value of such teachings, and who consented to hand it down as a Secret Doctrine, rather than declare it to a people and nation who were composed of two classes: those who were related to a bigoted and intolerant priesthood, and those who were kept in brutal ignorance by their direction. For neither class was the reconstituted philosophy in the least likely to be of value, and so was very properly kept in private hands. But not forever, for as the centuries have rolled on, many treatises by members of this Order have appeared, and have thrown light upon their doctrines. I should specify such works as those of Fludd, Michael Maier, Eugenius Philalethes, and Ragon.

These works may be to us almost incomprehensible, but they treat of man as a Soul and Spirit rather than as a body, and wherein their doctrines resemble any earlier ones, they are of Neo-Platonic type. Couple with this consideration the fact that these men lived lives of purity and zeal, meeting with no condemnation except from the clergy, whose bounden duty of course it was to censure all study of Man and his relations to the Divine, which extended beyond the path of their orthodoxy; and so far as you are orthodox perhaps you ought also to pass by on the other side of the Rosicrucians, for although they called themselves True Christians, few others did so; but then of course I am not forgetting that we are all supporters of this great undenominational Society of Benevolence, whose former rulers intentionally struck out all the Christian allusions in its Rituals only so lately as 1813, from which date, according to our deceased brother Whymper, "*We have what is a mere theistic confession of belief.*" There is no hint in any Rosicrucian tract that its students neglected the Christ ideal; but they were condemned for their Gnosticism which recognized the Christ Spirit as Divine, but did not identify it with the great Master Jesus, whom they deemed the teacher inspired by the Christ Spirit. It is, I believe, not so seriously denied by any one that Freemasonry before 1800 was a society avowedly Christian, as well as being composed of professing Christians, so that on this ground, for one, there is some reason for the suggestion that the early Freemasons were related to the Rosicrucians.

The crux of the whole matter before us is the early relation between the Societies, if any; and now there dawns upon you, possibly, the utter impossibility of ever demonstrating conclusively either the relation, or an entire distinction between Freemasonry and Rosicrucianism.

The difficulties are obvious and irremovable. It is hard enough to show evidence of relation between institutions, which existed in a distant past, even when both were famous openly and each endeavored to make itself known. Tell me, for example, how condemnation for offences passed from the power of a king or noble to that of a jury: or all the ties by which the Copernican system of the heavens was related to the Ptolemaic before it, and the Newtonian after it.

In the discussion before us, on the other hand, the utmost secrecy has been aimed at. By the Freemasons, their rituals have been kept private by terrible threats against any who should reveal them, even if they have not been careful to hide the existence of their Institution; but it is asserted that the Rosicrucians not only preserved the secrecy of their rituals and doctrines, but that they made the utmost endeavors to hide even the existence of the association, and for 120 years even the existence of individual members, and so well has the object been attained, that although the date of Christian Rosycross is 450 years ago, and that solitary students claiming to be successors, have appeared under the style of Frater R.C. every few years since, and although one such was certainly seen in Germany only 30 years ago, yet only today I have received a letter from a member of this Lodge, who has studied all that is current as to the Rosicrucians, this letter stating that he is not inclined to accept the statement that there ever was a Rosicrucian. But this is, of course, somewhat a question of words, no one denies that one who adopts the theory of development by the survival of the fittest, has a perfect right to call himself so far a Darwinian; so no one has a right to deny even to me the right to call myself a Rosicrucian, if I follow the precepts of a book published 350 years ago and written by a person who gave the name of Christian Rosenkreuz. I believe that there is every whit as much evidence this C. R. wrote the tractate, "*Chymische Hochzeit*," one of the so-called Rosicrucian books, as that Paul wrote the Epistle to the Hebrews, and a great deal more than there is to show that the drama "Titus Andronicus " was written by Shakespeare and not by Bacon. If you say, I will not believe that any man who has called himself a Rosicrucian during the last 300 years, was really admitted into the Secret Society of one C. R. who died in 1484, unless you can show me an official entry of the existence of his Lodge in the Records of some Town Hall, and a Record of his admission in a Roll which the British Museum authorities or Bro. Rylands will testify to be of the stated date; then of course there is an end of the matter, and there is no earthly use in discussing the subject. If you take the ground that no Society ever existed, whose records are not extant, or whose fame is not recorded in history, or whose secrets were not given away by an erring member, then also I am wasting my time and yours also. But the definiteness of evidence must be allowed to vary with the conditions of the matter sought to be established.

If I were to tell you, that unknown to anyone here present, and entirely unsuspected by anyone, there is now meeting regularly in this country a group of students who *call themselves* Rosicrucians; who were certainly some of them admitted by a form by older members who have since died, some of them thirty years ago; and that these seniors told those whom they admitted that they were admitted by the same form forty years before, and if these persons still study the doctrines of the books attributed to one C.R. of the date 1450 and that they can show you an intelligible sense in them, which you, the last product of modern education, cannot make out for yourselves, then I say that is evidence enough for me of the continued existence of such an Association, as is suggested by the "*Fama Fraternitatis Societatis, C.R.,*" first printed in 1614 in Germany.

But then Rosicrucians never ask anyone to accept statements as facts, and I don't advise you to believe a word they have said, unless you can get corroboration, because if you did accept such statements on my or their "*ipse dixit*" you would become a subject for ridicule to the cultured critic. Personally, I do believe that a student who took as a motto the initials C.R., and used as a device a Rose and a Cross, and became a learner in Eastern lore, did found a Society whose descendants still exist; but then I have what I deem corroboration, which I cannot make manifest, any more than you can go across the way, and explain Masonic ritual or modes of salutation.

Masonry a hundred years ago was Christian, in a sense at any rate, and Rosicrucian doctrine is Christian upon the face of it. This is one bond of alliance, and there are others. The great principles of Freemasonry are stated to be Brotherly Love, Relief and Truth; now these are merely names for purposes which are found in the oldest Rosy Cross books to be their aims and objects: see their "*Fama et Confessio, 1615.*" Firstly, they were notable as separating themselves largely from the world and calling themselves Frater, or brother in the Latin tongue, and they also called their instructor Father, which implies Brotherhood. Secondly, they were all pledged to relief of the suffering, to attempt the "*cure of diseases and that gratis*" (*Fama*), "*and to found hospices and retreats*" (*Espagnet*). Thirdly, they spent their lives in the search for truth, the knowledge of man, and his possibilities, and his relation to the other planes of existence beyond the material world, even up to the Divine ideal. (*See Michael Maier, "Themis aurea."*)

If many pupils failed to succeed in these high aims, so do many Freemasons fail in their objects; and the blame for such failure is not to be laid to the fault of either institution, but to the weakness of human nature.

The earliest known reference to the Rosicrucians in literature is dated Cassel, 1614. There then appeared an anonymous printed book, entitled, "*Fama Fraternitatis benedicti Ordinis Rosae-Crucis,*" or in English, "*The History of the Fraternity of the meritorious order of the Rosy Cross, addressed to the learned in general and to the governors of Europe.*" There is evidence that this work was circulated in MSS. in 1610. It narrates the history of a man who was brought up in a German monastery, and left Europe with a member of a Christian fraternity upon a journey to the Holy Land; this occurred, as we can decide by collateral evidence, about the year 1393. His fellow traveler died in Cyprus, and he then proceeded from place to place upon his own account, visiting Damascus, parts of Egypt, and Fez, and seeking out in each place those who were learned. He studied with them the old philosophies of Alexandria, and the Hebrew Kabala, and the remains of the ancient Egyptian Mysteries.

Returning to Europe he visited Spain, through which country owing to the invasions by Arabs and Moors, very much of the sources of the science of mediaeval Europe was derived;

for the Arabs, almost alone for centuries, made any attempt at organized study of nature and art, all Christendom lying during these same centuries in a dark and ignorant condition. At length he returned to Germany in 1402, and collected around him all those found to be congenial to philosophic study, — then deemed by the clergy to be magical if not devilish. To secure freedom from interference they took the only possible course of selecting a retired spot and keeping themselves to themselves. Here they founded this Society, and it was named after the motto, and perhaps the real name of their founder — Christian Rosenkreuz. Here they studied in privacy all the philosophy and science their chief had collected; and this, it is suggested, they cast into a coherent form and body of doctrine, and founded thereon certain practical applications. After living to about the year 1484, the master died, and his body was embalmed and enshrined in a vault decorated with mystical devices, and the whole closed up and hidden by a few of his first pupils, from those who were but neophytes. C.R. appears to have expressed a wish that his tomb and his Society should remain an entire secret for 120 years, after which time a certain exposure of the existence of a society and body of doctrine should be made known to learned men. His survivors then erected an inscription upon the vault door:

"*Post centum viginti annos patebo.*"

There is no need from the original wording of the book (*not the English version*) to suppose that this was anything more than a request, no need to look upon it as a prophecy. The elders of the little fraternity could hand down the tradition, and when the period ended the survivor would proceed, as is stated, to alter something of the building, and with the help of all other members, as the record states, certain parts were demolished, and the vault door found with its inscription.

This would bring us to 1604. The vault was entered and the ornate tomb of the great Master displayed to the view; the tomb was opened and the embalmed body discovered; there is nothing incomprehensible in this, for C. R. had visited and studied among Egyptian sages, who may presumably have kept to some extent the secret of the mode of embalming, now almost entirely lost.

The only part of the story really improbable is the assertion that *"into this vault the sun did not shine, yet was it illuminated by another sun (or light) situated in the flat heptagonal ceiling."* If this meant that an Everburning Lamp was there found, most persons now-a-days would doubt it, and yet there is a very large mass of references to such an invention to be found in old Latin literature, and there must have been some foundation for them. We must remember that there are certainly other inventions, which were once in use, and have been entirely lost, such as the mode of making the Tyrian purple dye.

The old tract continues with a lengthy description of the beauties of this burial place, and with its curious contents, and concludes with a short statement of the aims and concerns of the Society, adding a suggestion that the time of absolute secrecy having expired, more suitable persons would be admitted to the Society to study its philosophy and practice, but warning those who were self seekers and money getters that they would gain nothing from such an Order, nor obtain admission thereto.

Very soon afterwards, perhaps even in the same year, but certainly in 1616, this "*Fama*" was reprinted, and with it another tractate the "*Confessio Fraternitatis*," a statement of the doctrines of the Society, and without the history: but the doctrines and notions expressed in this second work are not simply those of the earlier one more fully set out. If there is one thing clear it is that in the "*Fama*" there is no reference to the Reformed Church, while in the "*Confessio*," the whole tone is Lutheran. Now the chief work of the Reformation took place between 1510-1560; that is between the assumed dates of closure and re-opening of the vault.

The "*Fama*" treats of their form of Christianity as contrasted to Mohammedanism and Pagan worship, while in the "*Confessio*" there is an adoption of Lutheran views as contrasted with those of Roman Catholicism: from this change of attitude and from the different style of the two texts I conclude that although one man may have published and edited both tracts yet it is certain that one mind did not, compose both. This is a point that all the critics seem to me to have missed, and there were about 600 of them within the first fifty years after publication of the "*Fama*," to say nothing of later authors such as Naude, and later still Nicolai, Buhle, de Quincey, and our Bro. Gould, and most recent of all Mr. A. E. Waite.

There has been a general consensus of opinion among the learned that of all the authors extant in Germany from 1600-1620, there was no one more notable as a theologian, mystic, and reformer than Johann Valentin Andreas, abbot of Adelburg and almoner to the Duke of Wirtemburg, and so he has been fixed upon by modern critics as the author; and I have no quarrel with those who assert he published these tracts, and that he wrote the "*Confessio*;" but if so, I deny that he wrote the "*Fama*," although it may have been put into his hands for publication. I see nothing unreasonable in supposing that such a mystic student should have been admitted to such a fraternity, and that he should have been told off to publish a partial expose of the system, if such a course was resolved upon. It is equally clear that if this were so, he having published these books by order, anonymously, would not subsequently have acknowledged the authorship, without orders to that effect.

The production of these tracts caused an immediate and most noteworthy stir in the world of the learned. Intense interest was excited, and the land was flooded with pamphlets against and for the existence and bona fides of such an institution. Those in favor of the Society were of course from men desirous of being received therein, while those which opposed it were equally naturally from the clergy who signed their names to their pamphlets with a long string of ecclesiastical titles of dignity. The philosophic students who sought admission to this mystic order signed and published their tracts with pseudonyms and so endeavored to keep themselves from persecution, trusting I suppose in the occult arts of the rulers of the Society to identify the authors and so receive them. Nothing whatever is known as to who were received and who were refused. But it is very clear that many pretenders to theosophy were not admitted, for of those who wrote patronizingly of the "*Fama*" and sought admission, several subsequently wrote other pamphlets against the Order, publishing the fact of their disappointment at non-admission, and implying a sneer at a Society which could refuse such eligible candidates.

From this time, although the existence of such a Rosicrucian fraternity of students was published, and although from time to time tracts were published upon the aims of the Society, and upon theosophic, alchymic, and mystical subjects, and signed by authors who either definitely claimed to be Rosicrucians or signed their mottoes or names as such, yet there has been no further revelation concerning the Society as a whole, or about its places of meeting: simply from that time onward, now here and now there, we hear of members of this curious band of students, and as I said some time back, we still hear of persons of such characteristics as we might naturally suppose the successors of C. R. to be.

The publication of the "*Fama*," or History of C. R. raised, as I have said, intense interest, and several editions of the book quickly followed each other; at Cassel in 1614, at Frankfurt in 1615, a Dutch version in 1616; in three years there were five German editions. Buhle says that after this first rage for the work there were many other editions. Later on it was translated and published in England by Thomas Vaughan, better known as Eugenius Philaletlies, in 1652; he was a notable member of the Order and wrote many books in Rosicrucian language and symbolism. An account of this famous chemist and mystic is found in Anthony A' Wood's *Athenae Oxonienses, vol. iii*. This author plainly states Vaughan to have been a Rosicrucian. In the same work is a reference to another notable Frater, Elias Ashmole, whom even my Bro. Gould acknowledges to have been an initiate into this German Society. Another contemporary was Sir Robert Moray, Founder of the Royal Society.

Still another, and perhaps the most important of all English Rosicrucians at that — or any later time — was Robertus de Fluctibus, or Fludd, a graduate in medicine, who travelled abroad and was initiated there: he published in 1616 a defense of the Society, named "*Apologia compendiaria Fraternitatem de Rosea-Cruce suspicionis et infamise maculis aspersam, abluens.*"

It is to be noticed that this English defense of Rosy Cross was long precedent to the first English translation of the "*Fama*"; this suggests that the book, doctrine, and Society, were well known in England quite apart from the printed and published history.

John Heydon, another physician, was also a contemporary, but he probably never passed beyond the low grades of the Order. The *Encyclopedia Metropolitana* states definitely that there was a London College of Rosicrucians in 1630. In Germany the most notable of the members who taught the esoteric side of the Rosicrucian spiritual philosophy of the Divine was Jacob Boehme. He published, in 1612, his great work, "*Aurora, or the Rising of the Sun*;" this is still, I was informed by Mackenzie, the name of a series of grades of the Society. Following Boehme came Gifftheil, Wendenhangen, Zimmerman, Frankenburg and Peter Mormius; some works of all of these authors are extant.

Another very famous member was Michael Maier, who took up for study especially the alchymic branch; several of his Rosicrucian tracts are even now procurable, such as "*Themis aurea, hoc est de legibus Fraternitatis R.C. Tractatus*," 1618, and "*Atalanta fugiens*."

These details have been given to show that from 1610-1700 there were given to the world a vast number of books of three classes; such as taught Rosicrucian doctrines; such as supported the truth of the published history of the Society; and lastly books which condemned the philosophy and religion of the Rosicrucians, and cast suspicion upon the truth of the history of the founding of the Order. I have shown that the members and writers of the Society were notable in England as well as in Germany.

I have hinted at, but have not gone at length into, the fact that the Rosicrucians acknowledged that any learning they had, was a rechauffe of Greek, Arabic, Chaldee, Hebrew and Egyptian systems, and was not any new thing. Consequently we had — at the period when Masonry ceased to be a Trade Guild, and became a Society for the admission of the gentry and learned — present in London certain men who were members of this curious Literary German Society of Mystics and Hermetists; we find also that these eminent English Rosicrucians were exactly the men whose initiation into the Masonic Guild just before it became literary or speculative, is well proven; for Vaughan was probably initiated about 1641; Elias Ashmole the Antiquary in 1646, and Sir Robert Moray in 1641, as is not disputed, and as is plainly stated in Anthony A' Wood's *Athenae Oxonienses*.

You have no proofs to give me of the exact years in which the principal philosophic and mystical allusions became embedded in the Masonic ritual, but there are many of you who believe the Ritual of Speculative Masonry formed a concrete whole in 1717, your grand landmark of the Order. I contend then that Ashmole and Vaughan possessed just such ancient lore as is found suggested in Masonic Ritual, that they did enter our Society, and that if it were not they who designed the ritual of Speculative Masonry in its present form with its quaint Kabalistic and Egyptian allusions, the fact is more amazing than the suggestion that they did so design it.

I will not enter at all into what I conceive to be plain, viz., that one source of our present organization was the institution of Trade Guilds; I am alone concerned with the origin of the classical, philosophic and mystic allusions in our rituals and ceremonies. I am content with Bro. Gould's dictum at p. 60 of vol. ii. of his *History of Freemasonry*. — He writes, "*it is clear that the Masonic body had its origin in the trades unions of mediaeval operatives,*" — just so, but that statement throws no light on the origin of our Masonic Ritual, in which the terms of operative art are almost restricted to the Explanation of the Working Tools; while other symbolism, entirely apart from the building arts, is so prominent.

This other symbolism is exactly of the nature that our Rosicrucians were capable of supplying, and my contention is that they did supply it.

In conclusion then, brethren, I consider that our existent Speculative Masonry was derived from two parents, and was gradually perfected from materials drawn from these two sources; from the Trade Guilds it obtained its organization and first nominal chiefs; its historic traditions of masonry being coeval with the erection of stately edifices, and the general craft symbolism of its ritual; while from the Rosicrucians, whose philosophy had at that time (*1650-1700*) been made more popular and less esoteric, it derived all the moral philosophy, its semi-Christian ideals, and its halo of mystic secrecy. Further upon the necessarily predominant ideal of the trade guild, mutual support and protection, was grafted from the same Rosicrucian source the newly formulated but old existing ideals of universal benevolence and the search after those real truths which underlie our humanity, and have been so grievously hidden beneath our forms of religion and civilization.

# THE ROSICRUCIAN AND HERMETIC BRETHREN

## By Hargrave Jennings

The following passages occur in a letter published by some anonymous members of the R.C., and are adduced in a translation from the Latin by one of the most famous men of the order, who addressed from the University of Oxford about the period of Oliver Cromwell; to which university the great English Rosicrucian, Robert Flood, also belonged, in the time of James the First and Charles the First. We have made repeated visits to the church where Robert Flood lies buried.

'Every man naturally desires superiority. Men wish for treasures and to seem great in the eyes of the world. God, indeed, created all things to the end that man might give Him thanks; But there is no individual thinks of his proper duties; he secretly desires to spend his days idly, and would enjoy riches and pleasures without any previous labor or danger. When we' (professors of abstruse sciences) 'speak, men either revile or contemn, they either envy or laugh. When we discourse of gold, they assume that we would assuredly produce it if we could, because. they judge us by themselves; and when we debate of it, and enlarge upon it, they imagine we shall finish by teaching them how to make gold by art, or furnish them with it already made. And wherefore or why should we teach them the way to these mighty possessions? Shall it be to the end that men may live pompously in the eyes of the world; swagger and make wars; be violent when they are contradicted; turn usurers, gluttons, and drunkards; abandon themselves to lust? Now, all these things deface and defile man, and the holy temple of man's body, and are plainly against the ordinances of God. For this dream of the world, as also the body or vehicle through which it is made manifest, the Lord intended to be pure. And it was not purposed, in the divine arrangement, that men should grow again down to the earth. It is for other purposes that the stars, in their attraction, have raised man on his feet, instead of abandoning him to the "all fours" that were the imperfect tentatives of nature until life, through the supernatural impulse, rose above its original condemned level--base and relegate.

'We of the secret knowledge do wrap ourselves in mystery, to avoid the objurgation and importunity or violence of those who conceive that we cannot be philosophers unless we put our knowledge to some ordinary worldly use. There is scarcely one who thinks about us who does not believe that our society has no existence; because, as he truly declares, he never met any of us. And he concludes that there is no such brotherhood because, in his vanity, we seek not him to be our fellow. We do not come, as he assuredly expects, to that conspicuous stage upon which, like himself, as he desires the gaze of the vulgar, every fool may enter; winning wonder, if the man's appetite be that empty way; and, when he has obtained it, crying out "Lo, this is also vanity!"

Dr. Edmund Dickenson, physician to King Charles the

Second, a professed seeker of the hermetic knowledge, produced a book entitled, *De Quinta Essentia Philosophorum:* which was printed at Oxford in 1686, and a second time in 1705. There was a third edition of it printed in Germany in 1721. In correspondence with a French adept, the latter explains the reasons why the Brothers of the Rosy Cross concealed themselves. As to the universal medicine, *Elixir Vitæ*, or potable form of the preternatural *menstruum*, he positively asserts that it is in the hands of the 'Illuminated', but that, by the time they discover it, they have ceased to desire its uses, being far above them; and as to life for centuries, being wishful for other things, they decline availing themselves of it. He adds, that the adepts are obliged to conceal themselves for the sake of safety, because they would be abandoned in the consolations of the intercourse of this world (if they were not, indeed, exposed to worse risks), supposing that their gifts were proven to the conviction of the bystanders as more than human; when they would become simply intolerable and abhorrent. Thus, there are excellent reasons for their conduct; they proceed with the utmost caution, and instead of making a display of their powers, as vainglory is the least distinguishing characteristic of these great men, they studiously evade the idea that they possess any extraordinary or separate knowledge. They live simply as mere spectators in the world, and they desire to make no disciples, converts, nor confidants. They submit to the obligations of life, and to relationships--enjoying the fellowship of none, admiring none, following none, but themselves. They obey all codes, are excellent citizens, and only preserve silence in regard to their own private convictions, giving the world the benefit of their acquirements up to a certain point: seeking only sympathy at some angles of, their multiform character, but shutting out curiosity wholly where they do not wish its imperative eyes.

This is the reason that the Rosicrucians passed through the world mostly unnoticed, and that people generally disbelieve that there ever were such persons; or believe that, if there were, their pretensions are an imposition. It is easy to discredit things which we do not understand--in fact, nature compels us to reject all propositions which do not consist with our reason. The true artist is supposed to avoid all suspicion, even on the part of those nearest to him. And granting the possibility, of the Rosicrucian means of the renewal of life, and supposing also that it was the desire of the hermetic philosopher, it would not be difficult for him so to order his arrangements as that he should seem to die in one place (to keep up the character of the natural manner of his life), by withdrawing himself, to reappear in another place as a new person at the time that seemed most convenient to him for the purpose. For everything, and every difficult thing, is easy to those with money; nor will, the world inquire with too resolute a curiosity, if you have coolness and address, and if you have the art of accounting for things. The man of this order also is *solus*, and without wife or children to embarrass him in the private disposition of his affairs, or to follow him too closely into his by-corners. Thus it will be seen that philosophers may live in the world, and have all these gifts, and yet be never heard of--or, if heard of, only as they themselves wish or suggest.

As an instance of the unexpected risks which a member

of this order may run if he turns his attention to the practical side of his studies, spite of all his precautions, we may cite the accident which happened to a famous Englishman, who disguised himself under the name of Eugenius Philalethes, but whose real name is said to be Thomas Vaughan. He tells us of himself, that going to a goldsmith to sell twelve hundred marks' worth of gold, the man told him, at first sight, that it never came out of the mines, but was the production of art, as it was not of the standard of any known kingdom: which proved so sudden a dilemma to the offerer of the gold, that he withdrew immediately, leaving it behind him. It naturally follows from this, that it is not only necessary to have gold, but that the gold shall be marketable or acceptable gold, as otherwise it is utterly useless for the purposes of conversion into money in this world. Thomas Vaughan, who was a scholar of Oxford, and was vehemently attacked in his lifetime, and who certainly was a Rosicrucian adept if there ever was one, led a wandering life, and fell often into great perplexities and dangers from the mere suspicion that he possessed extraordinary secrets. He was born, as we learn from his writings, about the year 1612, which makes him a contemporary of the great English Rosicrucian, Robert Flood; and what is the strangest part of his history, as we find remarked by a writer in 1749, is, that he is 'believed by those of his fraternity' (so the author adds) 'to be living even now; and a person of great credit at Nuremberg, in Germany, affirms that he conversed with him a year or two ago. Nay, it is further asserted' (continues the author) 'that this very individual is the president of the Illuminated in Europe, and that he sits as such in all their annual meetings'. Thomas Vaughan, according to the report of the philosopher Robert Boyle, and of others who knew him, was a man of remarkable piety, and of unstained morals. He has written and edited several invaluable works upon the secrets of the philosophers, some of which are in our possession; advancing very peculiar theories concerning the seen and the unseen. These books were disbelieved at the time, and remain discredited, principally because they treat of eccentric and seemingly impossible things. It is, however, certain that we go but a very little way out of the usual learned track before we encounter puzzling matters, which may well set us investigating our knowledge, and looking with some suspicion upon its grounds, spite of all the pompous claims of modern philosophers, who are continually, on account of their conceitedness, making sad mistakes; and breaking down with their plausible systems.

'Progress and enlightenment are prerogatives to which no generation in particular can lay a special claim', says a modern writer, speaking of railways and their invention. 'Intelligence like that of the Stephensons is born again and again, at lengthened intervals; and it is only these giants in wisdom who know how to carry on to perfection the knowledge which centuries have been piling up before them. But the age in which such men are cast, is often unequal to appreciate the genius which seeks to elevate its aspiration. Thus it was in 1820 that Mr. William Brougham proposed to consign George Stephenson to Bedlam, for being the greatest benefactor of his time. But now that we have adopted somewhat fully his rejected ideas of steam-locomotion and high rates of speed, which were with so much difficulty forced upon us, we complacently call ourselves "enlightened"; and doubtless we are tolerably safe in doing so, considering that the Stephensons, and similar scientific visionaries, no longer live to contradict us.' We might add, that the Rosicrucians hold their critics in light esteem--indeed in very light esteem.

If such is the disbelief of science of everyday use, what chance of credit has the abstruser knowledge, and those assertions of power which contradict, our most ordinary ideas of possibility? Common sense will answer, None at all. And yet all human conclusions and resolutions upon points which have been considered beyond the possibility of contradiction have been sometimes at fault. The most politic course is not too vigorously to take our stand upon any supposed fixed point of truth, but simply to admit that our knowledge is limited, that absolute truth is alone in the knowledge of God, and that no more truth is vouchsafed to man than he knows how to utilize: most of his uses, even of his little quantum of truth, being perverted. He must await other states for greater light, and to become a higher creature--should that be his happy destiny. As to certainty in this world, there is none--nor can there be any. Whether there is anything outside of man is uncertain. Hume has pointed out that there is no sequence between one and two. Other philosophers have ingeniously detected that our senses are all one, or all none. Man is the picture painted upon external matter, and external matter is the individuality that surveys the picture. In the world of physics, colors are tones in other senses, and tones are colors; sevenfold in either case, as the planetary powers and influences are septenary--which, in the ideas of the Rosicrucians, produce both.

# ROSICRUCIAN THOUGHTS ON THE EVER-BURNING LAMPS OF THE ANCIENTS

## By William Wynn Westcott

The ordinary Englishman of to-day considers the idea of a lamp which should be everburning only less absurd than the idea of perpetual motion. To the dabbler in modern science it is but little less absurd, but to the deepest thinkers, and to Rosicrucians, a scintillula of light appears on this mysterious subject. The true adept has discovered that although Nature is bound in general laws which seem universal, yet in Nature herself evidence may be found, when properly searched for, that at certain times and seasons, and in certain modes, unknown to us, her laws are over-ridden and replaced by a power to which she, the mighty mother, has herself to bow. The pages of the history of the world present to us many instances of such events, which we generally class as miracles; some of them are as well authenticated as any points in ancient history. The Israelitic passage of the Red Sea, the swallowing of Jonah by a whale which brought him forth again alive, and the Ascension of Jesus, are examples. The power of prophesy is a contradiction of the ordinary powers of earthly beings, and is so far miraculous. Angel visitors come but rarely now from the realms of glory; is heaven more distant? Or have men grown cold? Rosicrucians are nothing if not Christians, and Christians have ever believed in miracle, or have ever acknowledged the existence of an Omnipotence who can act at times in such a manner as to leave the traces and steps of the process so hidden as to tempt scoffers to doubt, and doubters to scoff.

But although perpetual motion be but a dream to us earthbound mortals, we do not doubt a future perpetual existence, and it is as reasonable to picture to ourself a perpetual flame, as an Eternity of Life. The ancient Egyptian priests pictured life as a flame. The Great Master of the Temple of this world being omnipotent, and able to do all things, does not usually proceed by miracles, or they will not be prized as such; an essence of miracle is rarity, a miracle imitated is not a second miracle. Ordinary events, then, being the extreme of opposition to miracle, there are yet events of a third and intermediate type, marvels, which cannot be understood of the people, but which are yet the product of a special gift to certain men, their spirits, minds, and bodies, who by due, careful, and sufficient training, wisdom and experience, have earned such a reward.

Such should the typical Rosicrucian be, a terrestrial earthly Body, the Temple in which dwells a mind trained to understand the powers of Nature, and enshrined within this, as a canopy, should sit a Divine afflatus, a portion of the Spirit of God, an ala of the Celestial Dove who brooded over the chaos, and this spirit may by patent submission to Deity, and by active efforts at power, draw down to itself a commission to work wonders, and so do "not as other men do."

The great tendency of the modern times has been to reduce all men to a level, a dead level, of mediocrity, an effort fatal to the supremacy of individuals, and which has tended to discourage research into the Hidden Mysteries of Nature and Science, as opposed to the parrot-like study of what are known as modern sciences, a study of enormous value to mankind, but yet not the stepping stones on the direct road to Deity. History then narrates the lives of many men, who, from the exhibition of uncommon powers and transcendent abilities and wisdom, are pointed out as the possessors of what we may fairly call occult Inspiration, "Poeta nascitur non fit;" but I should add "Magus nascitur non solum fit." No accident of birth alone can make a Magician, but intensity of duly directed effort may do so in a certain number of persons with specially favorable mental powers. We may be all born with an equal right to existence; but it is absurd to say we are all to be chiefs or Magi, for, as we are told in the Master's Degree, "some must rule, and some obey."

In 1484 died Christian Rosenkreuz, our great prototype; he was such a man; by the dispositions he made, and the Society he designed, he shook the whole Christian world for a century of years, and laid the first stones of the edifice we are still building to-day. In his tomb, when it was opened by the Fratres, in 1604, or 120 years after his decease, were found, besides other mysterious articles, lamps of a special and peculiar construction; hence the study of Sepulchral Lamps is one particularly germane to us. The discovery of lamps in ancient sepulchres, in some cases extinguished, in others burning with brilliance, was no rarity in the middle ages; but the destroying hands of the Goth and the Vandal have left few ancient tombs for modern research to explore. We have to content ourselves

39

with the observations and reports of our forefathers, the narratives of Arabian, Roman, and mediaeval authors. No fewer than 170 such authorities have written on this subject. Many of these references, in Greek and Latin literature, to lucent bodies, phosphorescence, and "mystic lamps found in tombs," deserve study, and will repay perusal.

The Darkness of Death and the Darkness of the Tomb are, and have ever been, common phrases; no wonder, then, that the ancients sought to minimize it. Hence we find that the relatives of a deceased person were desirous of relieving the gloom hanging over the grave of a beloved wife, kind parent, or respected brother, by any means in their power.

To include in the tomb a lamp and leave it burning was a kindly attention, even if it burned but one short hour; it was an offering to Pluto, to the Manes; it kept away spirits of evil, and preserved peace to the dead man: this knowledge of the limited time such a lamp could possibly remain alight acted, doubtless, as a stimulus to the discovery of a means of prolonging the burning power of a lamp indefinitely, and if I read history aright, in at least a few instances, the problem has been solved; so far at any rate as the manufacture of a lamp which should burn until deranged by the barbarian invader of its precincts. I shall narrate a few examples, premising that these are instances of different modes of obtaining the desired effect; besides these instances the ancient Latin authors speak of the use as illuminants, not alone of lamps, but of natural lucent bodies, which would suffice to dispel the gloom to some slight extent. Such were the diamond, the carbuncle, the glowworm, the exposure of phosphorus to the air, the ignition of certain substances which burn alone without any wick or arrangement, such as camphor, which will burn even floating on water. The presence of a combustible gas, which issues from clefts in the rock in some mines and caverns, seems to have been known, and was probably taken advantage of by the ancient sages to enhance the mystery and majesty of their secret rites. It is very possible that some of the priests of old were aware of the lucent property of some forms of sulphide of calcium, which have attracted much attention the last few years, in the shape of luminous paint.

I will submit also that references exist in the history of remote ages to suggest the mysterious light now so freely handled and produced by electricity was not unknown to the ancient sages. Numa, King of Rome, studied electricity, and left pupils of his art, of whom we are told was his successor Tullus Hostilius, who was destroyed whilst endeavoring to draw down from heaven and coerce the electric fluid from thunder clouds, or, as they said, front Jupiter Tonans. Eliphaz Levi remarks-"It is certain that the Zoroastrian Magi had means of producing and directing electric power unknown to us." – "Historie de la Magie," p. 57. Mediaeval scholars have fully debated several points in regard to ever-burning lamps, but in all cases without arriving at any definite result; much erudition has been expended on the question whether a lamp found burning on breaking open a tomb was not ignited by the admission of air, and had not been actually burning until it was disturbed; there is modern evidence in favor of this view, from the analogy of some chemical experiments, as, for example, phosphorized oil is invisible in the dark when enclosed in a sealed vial, when this is opened a light pours forth. On the other hand, evidence exists that some of the lamps actually paled and went out when the cavern in which they were found was opened, as a fine metal wire made white-hot by electricity in a sealed glass vacuumed ceases to shine when the glass is broken; others again burned on and could hardly be extinguished by water or other means, until the arrangement of the lamp was broken.

Other authors, taking for granted that some of these lamps had burned for hundreds of years, have discussed the necessary relation between oil or liquid consumed and wick. With regard to wick, there are several names of substances proposed as incombustible; but they are probably only synonyms of one body, namely, asbestos, which is even now used in our gas fires. It does not consume, although kept constantly red hot with flames flickering over it. Other names for it were-

Asbestinum-Plutarch uses this term, Pliny, and Solinus, and Baptista Porta; Linum Asbestinum by Albertus Magnus.

Amiantus-By Pancirollus, and by Lucius Vives.

Plume Alum-See Cyclopaedia by E. Chambers, 1741, art. "Allum," and so called by Wecker, De Secretis, lib. 3, cap. 2, and Agricola.

Earth Flax-Dr. Plot uses this name.

Linum Vivum-Mentioned by Plutarch, also as Linum Carpasium and Lapis Carystius-see De Defectu Oraculorum, and Pausanias in his Atticus.

Salamander's Wool-So called by Friar Bacon and Joachimus Fortius.

The ancients, we know, did try incombustible metal wires as wicks; but found that oil would not pass up them, as it does up fibres of cotton or wool.-See "Philos. Transactions," No. 166, p. 806, of the year 1684.

In respect to the oil for the lamp, there is no consensus of opinion as to the nature of it; neither of the authorities who narrate the finding of the lamps describe it in any way, yet many Latin authors discuss it. Some speak of it as bituminous oil, derived from the earth, thus forecasting the recent extensive use of petroleum. None of them definitely associate it with any known animal or vegetable oil. Many mystic references are, however, made to the labors of the Alchemists, who thought it must be of the nature of an essential oil of Sol, the metal gold, to be derived from it by alchemic processes. Sol, they say, must be dissolved into an unctuous humor, or the radical moisture of Sol must be separated.-See "Wolfhang Lazius," lib. III., c. 8, and "Camden Brittania," p. 572. For, say they, inasmuch as gold is so pure that it bears repeated meltings without wasting, so if it be dissolved into an oily residuum, such should support fire without being consumed.

It may suitably be explained in this place that the oldest Alchemists held peculiar views on flame and fire. Fire was to them an element-one of four; there were two contraries in nature, three principles, and four elements. Fire, as such, should not need what we call fuel to consume; but only as a means of detaining it in a certain place.-See "Licetus, De Lucernis," cap. 20-21 and "Theophrastus." They said there may be a relation between fire and fuel of three sorts-if the strength of the fire exceed that of the humor, it presently burns out; if the humor be too strong for the fire, the fire departs; but if the radical strength of the humor and of the fire be co-equal, then, caeteris paribus, that fire would burn continually, until the surrounding states of radical moisture or natural heat should be altered by external circumstances, as if a flame be made to burn in a closed vault, it would depart when such was opened.

Rosicrucian and Alchemical doctrines, especially their views on the connection between Fire and Water, are brought into close apposition to the dogmas of the religion of the Hebrews in some portions, at least, of the sacred writings, notably in the volume of the "Maccabees," Book II., cap. I., where we are told that when the Jews were led captive into Persia, the priest took the Sacred Fire from the Altar, and hid it in a dry, hollow place. Many years after, in more favorable times, Nehemiah sent priests to fetch this fire, nothing doubting its existence; they found water only in its stead. Nehemiah caused an altar of sacrifice to be made of wood and other materials, and this water was poured upon them, before all the people; when the clouds of the sky passed away, and the sun appeared; then the water that had been poured over the sacrifice burst into flame. The connection between Fire and Water again becomes prominent when we note the miracle of

Elijah, who made a sacrificial altar, poured water on it, and fire from heaven burned up the water, on the occasion when he condemned the priests of Baal who could not do likewise.-See Kings I., cap. xviii. Blavatsky claims that at the present time the priests of the secret temples of the Buddhists in Tibet, India, and Japan, use asbestos as a wick in lamps, which burn continuously without replenishing. Trithemius, Libavius, his commentator, and Korndorf, about the year 1500, each composed a material, by chemical processes, which they professed would burn forever. Mateer, a reverend missionary, states that he knew of a great golden lamp in a hollow place inside a temple at Trevandrum, kingdom of Travancore, which he had the best authority for believing had burned continuously for 120 years. The Abbe Huc, a great traveler, states that he has seen and examined an Everburning Lamp.

By the Levitical Law-Lev. vi., v. 13-the fire on the altar of Jehovah was never to be allowed to go out; but we are not told that it was ever burning without supply. It has been suggested that if everburning lamps were ever known, they would have been found in this application; but we know that the sacred flame was allowed to go out, and was renewed from heaven on several occasions.-Lev. ix., 24; 2 Chron. vii., 1; 1 Kings xviii., 38. Other writers have taken the other side of the argument, viz., that the gift of a flame that would need no attention would have tended to idolatry, to which the Israelites were ever prone. The Chaldeans and Persians used to maintain a perpetual fire in the temples.

Certain scholars have considered that the "window" mentioned as placed in the Ark of Noah was not such, as during a period of prolonged cloud and storm a window should not light such a chamber. In the Hebrew version of Genesis, cap. 6, v. 16, the word is tzer, which means "something transparent," and is to be compared with the similar word zer, always translated "splendour" or "light," hence they suggest that this tzer, or zer, was some form of ever burning light, or "the universal spirit fixed in a transparent body," similar to the Mysterious Urim and Thummim.

Alchemy and its successor, Chemistry, are said to have originated in Egypt, that land of ancient marvels, and, indeed, these names are intimately related, the ancient name of Egypt being Chm or Land of Ham, from which the title Chymia, in Greek Chemi and Ges Cham is derived. The learned Kircher writes in A.D. 1650 that several travelers in Egypt found in his time Burning Lamps in the Tombs at Memphis. Numa Pompilius, King of Rome, who certainly experimented with the natural electricity of the clouds, built a Temple to the Nymph Egeria, and made in it a spherical dome, in which he caused to burn a Perpetual Flame of Fire in her honor; but in what manner this flame was produced we have no knowledge. Nathan Bailey, in his "Brittanic Dictionary," 1736, remarks that in the Museum of Rarities at Leyden, in Holland, there were two of these lamps, only partially destroyed. A lamp still burning was found during the Papacy of Paul III., about 1540, in a tomb in the Appian Way at Rome, supposed to be that of Tulliola, the daughter of Cicero. The tomb was inscribed: "Tulliolae Filiae Meae;" she died B.C. 44; it had burned over

1550 years, and became extinguished as soon as exposed to the air; the whole body was in perfect preservation, and was found floating in a vessel of oil. See "Pancirollus, Rerum Memorabilium Deperditarum," vol. I., p. 115, Franciscus Maturantius, Hermolaus, and Scardeonius.

Such a lamp is stated to have been found in 1401, in the reign of Hen. III., King of Castile, not far from Rome, on the Tiber, in the stone tomb of Pallas, the Arcadian, son of Evander, slain by "Turnus Rex Rotulorum" in the wars at the time of the building of Rome; nothing could extinguish the flame of this lamp until it was broken. On the tomb were the words: "Filius Evandri Pallas, quem lancea Turni militis occidit, mole sua jacet hic." -See "Martianus, Liber Chronicorum," lib. xii., cap. 67.

Two miles from Rome an inundation broke down a wall, and disclosed an ancient tomb; on the cover stone were the letters "P.M. R.C. cum Uxore;" in it an earthen urn was found; when fractured, a bituminous smoke issued; in the bottom was a lamp, which went out; the fragments were still oily; this became dry after exposure.-See "Lowthorp, Abridgment of Philos. Trans.," vol. III., sec. xxxv., also No. 185, p. 227.

In a certain temple of Venus in Egypt there hanged a lamp which neither rain nor wind could put out, says, St. Augustine, in his work "De Civitate Dei," lib. xxi., cap. 6, and he associates its make with Magic, and the Devil, as indeed do all Roman Catholic authorities whenever they mention any of these lamps. Fortunius Licetus describes this lamp in his work

"De Reconditis Lucernis Antiquorum," cap. vi., and see '"Isidorus, De Gemmis."

Ludovicus Vives, 1610, in his notes to St. Augustine, says that in his father's time, A.D. 1580, a lamp was found in a tomb, which from the inscription was 1500 years old; it fell to pieces when touched. This Commentator does not follow his master in his denunciation of these lamps, but says they must have been made by men of the greatest skill and wisdom.- See also "Maiolus, Episcopus, Colloquies."

At Edessa, or Antioch, in a recess over a gateway a burning lamp was found by the soldiers of Chosroes, King of Persia, elaborately closed in from the air. From a date inscribed it was known to have been placed there soon after the time of Christ, or 500 years before. Beside this lamp a crucifix was found fixed.-See "Fortunius Licetus," cap. vii., and Citesius in his "Abstinens Consolentanea." In the volcanic island of Nesis, near Naples, in the year 600 a marble tomb was found, and when opened it contained a vase in which was a lamp still alight; the light paled and soon was extinguished when the vase was broken. See "Licetus," cap. x. See "Baptista Porta, Magia Naturalis," lib. xii. cap. ult., A.D. 1658.

A very notable example occurred in the discovery of lamps buried in urns about A.D. 1500; they were taken possession of by Franciscus Maturantius, and described by him in a letter to Alphenus, his friend; they had been buried 1500 years. A labourer at Ateste, near Padua, in Italy, found a sepulchre, in which was a fictile urn, and within it there stood another urn, and in this smaller one a lamp burning brightly;

and on each side of it there was a vessel, or ampulla, each of them full a of pure fluid oil; one was made of gold, and the other one of silver. On the outer urn were these words engraved:-

Plutoni sacrum munus ne attingite fures, Ignotum est vobis hoc quod in urna latet Namque elementa gravi clausit digesta labore, Vase sub hoc modico Maximus Olybius. Adsit secundo custos sibi copia cornu Ne tanti pretium depereat laticis.

Thieves! Grasp not this gift sacred to Pluto, Ye are ignorant of what it contains hidden, For Maximus Olybius has enclosed in This small urn, elements digested with heavy toil, Let abundance be present in a second vase as a guardian to it, Lest the value of so much oil should perish.

On the smaller one were these words:-

Abite hinc pessimi Fures Vos quid vultis, vestris cum oculis emisitiis. Abite hinc, vestro cum Mercurio Petasato caduceato que Donum hoc Maximum, Maximus Olybius Plutoni sacrum facit.

Get ye hence, most wicked thieves, What do you desire with your rolling eyes? Get ye hence with your broad hatted Mercury Carrying a wand with twisted snakes. Maximus Olybius makes this, His greatest offering, sacred to Pluto. See "F. Licetus," cap. ix., and "Scardeonius, De Antiq. Urbis Patavinae; Rubeus, De Destillatione," and "Lazius, Wolfhang," lib. iii., cap.18. Hermolaus Barbarus, in his Corollary to

Dioscorides, speaks of a wondrous liquor to sustain combustion, known to Democritus and Trismegistus. Jacobus Mancinus wrote to Licetus that he knew of a burning lamp dug up from the Monte Cavallo at Rome; it was still burning when found, and within it was a bituminous substance.

Plutarch in his work "De Defectu Oraculorum," states that in a Temple to Jupiter Ammon a lamp stood in the open air, and neither wind nor rain put it out, and the priests told him it had burned continually for years.- See also "Licetus," cap. v. Herodotus tells us that the Egyptians made a special and extensive use of lamps in the religious festivals, and that the Temples of King Mycerinus had many mysterious ones. Strabo, and Pausanias in his Atticus, narrate that in the temple of Minerva Polias, at Athens, there was a mysterious lamp of gold always burning; it was made by Callimachus. The altar of the Temple of Apollo Carneus, at Cyrene, was similarly furnished. A like account is given of the great Temple of Aderbain, in Armenia, by Said Ebn Batric.

Kenealy in his "Book of God" calls attention to the name Carystios applied to the asbestine wicks of the lamps in ancient Greek temples, and draws attention to its relations to Chr. of Christos and to Eucharist, anointed with oil, as to everburning lamps before the throne, as in the Apocalypse.

Chrs.= [Hebrew: ChRSh]=solar fire.

Chre.= [Hebrew: ChRH]=sun=he burned.

Krs.= [Hebrew: KRSh]=sun=(Greek?-EO) Kupios=Cyrus.

Ceres=was called Taedifera=torch bearing.

Chrs., from this also comes Eros in Greek, material light coming from ineffable light. There is a curious reference of asbestos to fire, and the heat of the sun, in "The Ecstatic Journey to Heaven" of Kircher, where Casmiel, the genius of this world, gives Theodidaktos a boat of asbestos to embark in for his travels to and on the sun, the centre of heat. See "Itinerar 1, Dialogue 1," cap. 5.

Irish lore recounts a mysterious everburning flame in the Temple at Kildare, sacred to St. Bridget-Daughter of Fire.-See Giraldus Cambrensis, De Mirab. Hibern. 2, xxxiv.

Khunrath, in his "Amphitheatrum Sapientiae Aeternae," cites the ancient author of "The Apocalypse of the Sweet Spirit of Nature," as speaking of a liquid which burneth with a bright light and wastes not.

At the dissolution of the Monasteries in Britain, by order of Henry VIII., a tomb, in Yorkshire, purporting to be that of Constantius Chlorus, father of the Great Constantine, was opened and ransacked, and a lamp burning was found in it: he died 300 A.D.-See Camden "Brittania" (Gough's edition, III. p. 572.)

Lazius, in his "Comment. Reipub. Romae," writes that the Romans under the Empire possessed the secret of preserving lights in tombs by means of the oiliness of gold, resolved by their art into a fluid.-See lib. III., cap. 18.

An ancient Roman tomb was discovered in Spain, near Cordova, near the site of the ancient Castellum priscum; in this tomb was found a lamp. This lamp is described by Mr. Wetherell, of Seville. See an essay by Wray, "Athenaeum," Aug. 8th, 1846.

The last relation which I propose to cite to you is from Dr. Robert Plot, the Archaeologist, written in the time of Charles the Second, as follows:-

A certain man, engaged in digging, having at a particular spot turned up the earth deeper than usual, came upon a door, which he subsequently was able to open, and found beneath it a descending passage with steps; these he descended, and ultimately, with much trepidation and many delays, he arrived at the entrance of a vault.

This underground chamber was lighted up by a lamp, which was placed in front of a statue of a man in armor sitting at a table, leaning on his left arm; in his right hand was a sceptre or weapon.

When the intruder advanced, a portion of the floor moved with his weight, and the figure became raised up, at the next step the arm was elevated, and as the man took the third step the arm descended, shattering the lamp and extinguishing it. The man was terrified, and made a hasty retreat as soon as he recovered possession of his senses sufficiently to find his way out of the vault.

The place became famous for some time as the sepulchre of a Rosicrucian, and was regarded as a triumph of mystic skill and knowledge, which at once proved the possession of undreamed of powers in the designer, and yet provided the means of as certainly keeping his secret. See also "Spectator," No. 379, of 1712.

This essay has already extended beyond the contemplated limits, so I refrain from a long resume. These pages provide much food for thought. That lamps have burned for long periods of time untended is testified to by more than 150 authorities, and some dozen instances of this marvel are borne witness to by a large proportion of these authors.

From the time that has elapsed since everburning lamps were found, and from the comparative ignorance of the world at that period of the distant past, comes to our minds some hesitation and doubt as to accuracy of detail, and this is unavoidable. But the consensus of ancient opinion must point to the broad conclusion that there formerly existed an art that has been lost in the dim light of the dark ages of the world. Pancirollus catalogues many other such lost arts, and modern science is flung back baffled from the performance of many a deed which could have been freely done by the ancient sages.

Several of our most modern discoveries have been shown to have been anticipated by men who are contemptuously regarded by modern scientists. So it has ever been. Earth knows but little of its greatest men; its greatest men are but pigmies in the presence of time, antiquity, and futurity. "Knowledge comes, but wisdom lingers," said the poet laureate. The Christian Rosicrucian can only exclaim-

"Lead, kindly Light, lead thou me on; The night is dark, and I am far from home."

# THE TRUE ROSICRUCIAN ORDER

By Samuel Liddell MacGregor Mathers

The constant and unauthorized use of the title Rosicrucian by imposters of every kind, with the idea of thus filling their own pockets at the expense of those of the general public whom they may thus succeed in beguiling, has at length reached the proportions of a veritable nuisance. That is why I am writing this article as the External Head of the True Order. We are a secret Order, pursuing our studies in secret, and our Neophytes must be prepared not only to take, but also to keep a most solemn Oath of Secrecy as to our Rituals, Ceremonies, and Formulas, in which, however, there is nothing contrary to the civil, moral, or religious duties of the aspirant, also there is nothing to shock her or his self-respect. The grades follow in succession like the rungs of a ladder, or the steps of a staircase, each with its particular studies, its rituals, ceremonies and formulas, and its own particular Obligation of Secrecy. I have no doubt that at this point many of the readers of this article will at once say: "What is the use of all this secrecy and mystery; we Americans like truth and frankness and everything above board, etc., etc."

Now not alone does this attitude of mind render it more easy for the imposters to thrive at your expense, pretending to teach and reveal things which they never knew, but also it is apt to foster the idea that True Wisdom, that is to say the Occult Science of the Whole Universe can be easily fathomed and comprehended with little or no trouble! A state of ignorant arrogance of mind closely akin to, only far exceeding that of the man who is supposed to have said that he could play the violin quite well at first attempt although he had never learned it!

The human mind is far too influenced by the conceit that it is in a position to criticize anything, no matter how much larger and greater than itself; even the universal All and the ways of the Great Creator thereof, and attitude too much fostered by the teachings of the so-called Theosophy of the Present Day. There are several potent reasons for the practice of secrecy in the Mystic Studies and the Contemplations of our Order; foremost among which may be cited the importance of not placing in the hands of the multitude the knowledge of formulae which may be used for evil as well as for good, and this without any control.

Again, Truths which at best can only partially comprehended by those receiving them, owning to the lack of properly trained preparation become but pseudo-truths and consequently False Formulae, necessarily the more misleading and dangerous to a narrow and conceited metal scope of assimilation. Our Principal Objects of Study may be considered to include the acquirement of that Great Occult Wisdom, chiefly derived from Ancient Egyptian and Chaldean, which treats of God and of the Gods, of Spiritual Beings and Races, of the Secret Forces existing in Nature, of Life, of Death, of our Mystic Environment, etc. Every student set to solve a mathematical problem, learns that the first step is the stating in exact mathematical terms his or her exact extent of ignorance of the result to be attained. How many Occult Students are there, whoever think of applying this procedure to the attempt to solve the far graver problems of Occult Wisdom? Probably none.

They find it on the contrary much easier to throw the onus of their probable errors on to supposititious Mahatmas, brain-waves, impulses sent from suppositious "Grand Lodge" of "Masters," and what not at times these theories seem to work, and at other times they don't. It matter little, for the responsibility is thus duly accounted for! I do not say that certain Secret Chiefs and Masers do not exist, but what I do say is that an incalculable amount of nonsensical rubbish has been promulgated concerning them; even to the point of asserting that our Great and Ancient Order is under the control of the Theosophical Mahatmas, the which is a most utterly false a impertinent statement. We have a profound respect for Christianity, and are in no sense hostile to the Roman Catholic Church, nor yet to the other forms of Christian belief, provided that on the more Unitarian side they do not too far gravitate towards Atheism.

And we especially consider the Roman Catholic Church has resolutely preserved in its Ceremonies the August Symbols of the Divine Wisdom.

In our preliminary work we encourage our members rather to study the Greater World, than themselves who are the Lesser World, so as to counteract the natural tendency to become too self-centered, and to exalt the self at the expense of the Universal Nature. We only consider the question of re-incarnation later, and then in a far more exceptional, restricted, and different sense to that given to it by the ordinary Out Occultists of today.

Possessing as we do the True Knowledge of the Races of the Elements we consider most of the ideas promulgated concerning them as erroneous and misleading. We are not opposed to Religions other than the Christian, to which the early Egyptian Religion, long before the time of Moses, very closely approached, and among us are Members of many different Religions. Neither do we consider ourselves only beholden to the Mediaeval Branch of our Order established in Germany, for our Secret Knowledge; we consider it simply as a Branch of our Order and no more.

# THE ROSICRUCIANS

## By Willian Wynn Westcott

It is well at certain times to consider our status as Rosicrucians, and to remind ourselves of the origin of the Society to which we belong, to notice how far we moderns have strayed from the original paths laid down by our Founder, C.R., and to take a note of the kindred Societies of Rosicrucians which are now in being, so far as we know of them. With regard to past history we must not be surprised that extant published records are very scanty, for the purpose of the Rosicrucians was to be unknown to the people among whom they Lived.

Some few notable persons only appear to have had the right to function as recognized members of the Rosicrucian Colleges, for instance, Michael Maier the German student of Alchemy who died in 1662, and Dr. Robert Fludd of London and Bearstead near Maidstone who died in 1637. The Star of Rosicrucianism is now once more in the ascendant and our Society has made rapid strides in the past ten years. It is curious to note that waves of interest in occult and mystical subjects, seem to sweep over a nation at intervals; periods of Rosicrucian enlightenment alternate with other periods of materialistic dogmatism. We must remember that Rosicrucianism itself was "no new thing" but only a revival of still earlier forms of Initiation, and was a lineal descendant of the Philosophies of the Chaldean Magi, of the Egyptian priests, of the Neo-

Platonists, of the Hermetists of Alexandria of the Jewish Kabbalists and of Christian Kabbalists such as Raymond Lully and Pic de Mirandola.

The nominal Founder of our Society–Christian Rosencreuz, did not invent, at least in our modern sense of the word, the doctrines he promulgated, and which we should now study. It is narrated that he journeyed to Arabia, to Palestine, to Egypt and to Spain, and in the seats of learning in those countries he found and collected the mystic lore, which was made anew by him into a code of doctrine and knowledge. On his return from these foreign travels he settled in Germany, founded a Collegium, selected certain friends and transformed them into enthusiastic pupils, and giving his new Society his own name, he laid the foundation of that scheme of Mystical Philosophy, which we are now here to perpetuate and carry into practice: let us remember that he died in the year 1484, that is so far back as the reign of our King Richard the Third. The fratres of the original Collegium, who met in the "Domus Sanctus Spiritus," or " House of the Holy Spirit," were learned men, earnest students and public benefactors. Their rules were: That none of the members should profess any art except to relieve the sick and that gratis; each one should wear the ordinary dress of the country, and should attend on Corpus Christi day at a general Convocation every year, whenever possible to do so; each one should seek a suitable pupil to succeed him: that the secret mark of each one should be C.R or R.C., and that the Society should remain secret for 100 years.

As time went on the purposes and duties of the fratres became altered, the cure of the sick especially was taken over by the development of the medical profession. About 1710, one Sigmund Richter, using the motto of "Sincerus Renatus," published at Breslau his work called "The perfect and true preparation of the Philosophical Stone according to the secret of the Brotherhoods of the Golden and Rosy Cross." In this volume we find a series of 52 rules for the guidance of Rosicrucian members; these rules are such as were likely to lead to useful and orderly lives.

Again, about 1785, there was published at Altona in Germany a most important volume of colored theosophical plates with eludicatory words and phrases and several essays on Rosicrucian subjects: its title was "Geheime Figuren der Rosenkreuzer"; it was in two portions. An English translation of some part of this work was published in 1888 by Franz Hartmann, a German Theosophist. We catch a further glimpse of the purposes of the Rosicrucians at a later date, from a curious little tract relating to a French branch of the Society, which relates the Reception of Dr. Sigismund Bacstrom in the Mauritius—French colony—by the Comte de Chazal in 1794. I cannot say where the original MS. now is, but our copy was made by the secretary of the well-known Rosicrucian and crystal-gazer Frederick Hockley, who died in 1885. Bacstrom signed his pledge to fourteen promises;—to piety and sobriety, to keep the secrecy of his admission, to preserve the secret knowledge, to choose suitable successors, to carry on the great work, to give aid and charity privately, to share discoveries with his fellows, to avoid politics, to help strangers, and to show gratitude to those who had led to his reception; etc. During a recent visit to East Africa I met in Natal a Mauritius born doctor whose wife was a Miss de Chazal, a native of Mauritius; among her ancestors about 1780-90 there was this M. de Chazal who was an eccentric genius and was considered to possess curious arts; he also became a notable Swedenborgian and held classes of mystical philosophy.

The name is many times mentioned in a French history of Mauritius which was lent to me by Dr. Dumat of Durban. At the time of the French Revolution it would be natural for our count de Chazal to drop his title, as did many of the French nobility. The aim of our own Society at the present day is to afford mutual aid and encouragement in working out the great problems of Life, and in discovering the Secrets of Nature; to facilitate the study of the system of Philosophy founded upon the Kabbalah and the doctrines of Hermes Trismegistus, which was inculcated by the original Fratres Rosae Crucis. of Germany, A.D. 1450; and to investigate the meaning and symbolism of all that now remains of the wisdom, art and literature of the Ancient World.

The Rosicrucian Societies of Anglia, Scotia and the United States, alike Masonic bodies, are by no means the only descendants of the original Collegium, for in Germany, and Austria there are other Rosicrucian Colleges of more direct descent than our own, which are not fettered by any of the limitations which Freemasonry has imposed upon us, and some of these, although not composed of many members, include students who understand many curious phenomena, which our

Zelators have not studied. The German Rosicrucians keep their Colleges and membership entirely secret, they print no transactions nor even any notices, and it is almost impossible to identify any member. The German groups of Rosicrucians now existing are much more immersed in mystic and occult lore than ourselves; they endeavor to extend the human faculties beyond the material toward the ethereal, astral and spiritual worlds: at the present time I understand that they use no formulated Ritual, but German Colleges have experienced a notable revival and the teachings of Rudolf Steiner are considered as giving an introduction of their system of occult Theosophy. Several of Steiner's volumes are now available in English translations, such are his "Initiation and its Results," "The Gates of Knowledge," and "Way of Initiation." They are well worthy of study. The Societas Rosicruciana in Scotia, as well as the Societas Rosicruciana in the U.S.A. were branches from the same Rosicrucian source and sprang from a rejuvenation by Frater Robert Wentworth Little of that lapsed Rosicrucian College in England which is mentioned by Godfrey Higgins in his notable work "The Anacalypsis," or "An attempt to withdraw the Veil of the Isis of Sais," which was published in 1836; he remarks that he did not join the old College there referred to.

About fifty years earlier a certain eminent Jew named Falk, or Dr. Falcon, lived in London (a reference to whom will be found in the "Encyclopaedia of Freemasonry" by Kenneth Mackenzie) and was of high repute as a teacher of the kabbalah and of other studies of a Rosicrucian character; he was indeed said to have magical powers. Falk could not have fully affiliated to any Rosicrucian College because he was a strict Jew of the Jews, and the members of all true Rosicrucian Colleges have always been Christians, but perhaps not of an orthodox type, for there was a tendency in the teachings toward Gnostic ideals. Mackenzie classes Dr. Falk among the Rosicrucians of eminence, and certainly told me he had first hand evidence of his connection with the Society; many Christian students adopted a modification of the old Jewish kabbalah, so perhaps some Jews have been allied to the Christian Rosicrucians. Our own Magus Frater R. W. Little surrounded himself with several other notable Rosicrucian students, of whom I may mention the late Supreme Magus in Anglia, Dr. William Robert Woodman, a learned Kabbalist and Hebrew scholar; W.J. Hughan, the great Masonic historian; William Carpenter, editor of Calmet's "Dictionary of the Bible"; Alphonse Constant, better known as "Eliphaz Levi," who gave Fratres Little and Kenneth Mackenzie much assistance, and was in return elected an honorary member of the Metropolitan College in 1873.

Our Society unfortunately lost Frater Little at a very early age. Frater H. C. Levander, too, a Professor at University College, London, was a learned member; and took great interest in the mystic lore of the Society. The late Lord Lytton, the author of "Zanoni" and "The Strange Story," who was in 1871 Grand Patron of our Society, took very great interest in this form of Philosophy, although he never reached the highest degree of knowledge; for public reasons he once made a disavowal of his membership of the Rosicrucians, but he had been admitted as a Frater of the German Rosicrucian College at Frankfort on the Main; that College was closed after 1850.

Among the Fratres who have recently been ornaments to our Colleges, I may draw attention to the lately deceased and quaintly cultured John Yarker of Didsbury; to our late Adept of York, T. B. Whytehead, who was famous as an antiquarian: to Frater Fendelow of the Newcastle College, who was the author of a learned and suggestive Rosicrucian Lecture: to Frater F. F. Schnitger, who made deep researches into the French and German Rosicrucian Treatises: to Samuel Liddell Mathers, the translator of portions of the Hebrew "Zohar," and to Frederick Holland, the author of "The Temple Rebuilt," and "The Shekinah Revealed." Another deceased Frater of eminence was Benjamin Cox of Weston-super-Mare, and with him I naturally couple the greater name of Frater Major F. G. Irwin, who, however has now also gone to a Temple far away. Among the learned juniors of our Society, I may name Fratres Dr. Vaughan Bateson, Thomas Henry Pattinson, the Rev. C. E. Wright, Sir John A. Cockburn, W. J. Songhurst, Herbert Burrows, A. Cadbury Jones, W. Wonnacott, Dr. Wm Hammond, Dr. B. J. Edwards, and Dr. W. C. Blaker. Our Colleges need not languish for want of subjects of study; the narrative of the foundation of our Society is singularly suggestive of points for future investigation.

The German "Fama Fraternitatis" of 1614, in an English translation by Thomas Vaughan of 1652, presents you with the History of Christian Rosenkreuz: its companion tract the "Confessio Fraternitatis" gives you a slight insight into the views of the Rosicrucians of a date a hundred years later. The "Chymische Hochzeit" or "Chemical Wedding" by C.R., and the "Secret Symbols of the Rosicrucians" by F. Hartman, are tractates of Rosicrucian Allegory which will well repay, not only perusal, but deep study; while the elucidation of the whole set of Medieval Divinatory Sciences, Astrology, Geomancy, etc, are suitable themes for lectures in your College For such as can understand medieval Latin a most interesting work is the "Oedipus Aegyptiacus" of Athanasius Kircher. It is desirable that our students should make themselves acquainted with the Ancient Mysteries of Egypt, of Greece and of Rome. The basis of the Western occultism of medieval Europe is the Kabbalah of the medieval Hebrew Rabbis, to which I have published "An Introduction." This philosophy, although at first sight barbarous and crude, yet will be found, when one has grown familiar with the nomenclature, to be a concrete, coherent and far-reaching scheme of Theology, cosmology, ethics and metaphysics, serving to throw light on many obscure Biblical passages and to suggest original views of the meaning of most of the allegorical descriptions found in the Old Testament.

A copy of a very curious old Kabbalistic picture from a Syriac Gospel with a descriptive essay by Dr. Carnegie Dickson, a notable Scotch Rosicrucian Adept, has just been given to our Library. The works of the great Rosicrucian Kabbalist, Eliphaz Levi, are, to those who read French with ease, a mine of mystic lore, full of fine imagery, and replete with magical formulas. His "Histoire de la Magie" is a storehouse of information relating to the Secret Sciences and Secret Fraternities of all times and among many nations, while in English the two volumes of the new edition of Heckethorn's "Secret Societies" should he read as an introduction to deeper personal research. The work of Franz Hartmann, named "Magic, White and Black," I can recommend to serious enquirers, for it elucidates the real aims of the Higher Magic, with which alone we are concerned, and it clears away many misconceptions which exist in the minds of the uninitiated. To such as desire to follow more closely the Old Testament religious element, I should advise a perusal of the Commentaries of Dr. Allen Barnes on "Daniel" and "The Book of Revelation," and the symbolical descriptions of the book of Ezekiel. On the Christian aspect I recommend "The Perfect Way," or "The Finding of Christ," by the late Dr. A. Kingsford; in this volume will be found worked out the broader scheme of Christian teaching which is so apt to be obscured by sectarian forms of worship.

The tenets of this work are closely approximate to those of the earliest of the followers of Christian Rosencreuz, whose name was probably a mystic title, motto or synonym, and not a family cognomen:- "Christian" referring to the general theological tendency, and "Rosenkreuz" to the Cross of Suffering whose explanation and key may need a Rose or secret explanation. There is one doctrine for the learned, and a simpler formula for those who are unable to bear it yet, even as the new testament itself tells us, of the Great Master who taught his immediate disciples the true keys, but to others he spake only in parables,–"and without a parable spake he not unto them." Such, my Fratres, are suitable subjects for the attention of your members, but there are many allied topics which might form suitable centers of interest and instruction, for example the whole range of church architecture as crystalized symbolism, the dogmas of the Gnostics, the several systems of philosophy of the Hindus, the parallelism between Rosicrucian doctrine and Eastern Theosophy, for which read Max Heindel's "Rosicrucian Cosmo Conception," and that enticing subject, the origin and meaning of the 22 Trumps or symbolic designs of the "Tarocchi" or pack of Tarot cards, which Eliphaz Levi says form a group of keys which will unlock every secret of Theology and Cosmology. For such as are interested in the Alchemy of the past I recommend a perusal of "A Suggestive Enquiry into the Hermetic Mystery" 1850, by an anonymous author, and E. A. Hitchcock's "Remarks on Alchemy and the Alchemists," 1857. And, lastly, we may make researches into that most interesting problem—

Did Speculative Masonry arise from the Rosicrucians? I am to understand that the German Rosicrucians say that before the Masonic revival of 1717 these were identical in Europe. Let us not forget, that not only as Rosicrucians, but even as Freemasons, we are pledged, not only to Brotherhood and Benevolence, but also to look below the surface of things, and to seek and to search out the hidden secrets of Nature and of Science. Let us bear in mind that a little knowledge is a dangerous thing, but that deeper study reveals the roots of knowledge, as well as increases our store of information. Let us not, with folded arms, float with the tide of indolence, but ever strive after increase of that true knowledge which is wisdom and remember that "to labor is to pray," or as the Latin motto has it, "Laborare est Orare," for the day is coming to each one of us when no man can work, and the value of the work of each man will be tried in the balance of justice, and if we have done well we shall gain a rich reward.

www.ingramcontent.com/pod-product-compliance
Lightning Source LLC
LaVergne TN
LVHW041458070426
835507LV00009B/668